> >PRESS PLAY>

Published in Great Britain in 2023
by Big White Shed, Morecambe
www.bigwhiteshed.co.uk
Printed and bound by Imprint Digital, Devon
ISBN 978-1-915021-20-5/978-1-915021-23-6
Copyright © Haroon Khan
Cover Design by Jason Malipol

A CIP catalogue record of this book is available from the British Library.

Why would you hold it in when you got stories to tell?
So many lost odysseys stuck in your shelf.

Hawk House - Chill Pill (Experiment 2)

Haroon Khan's debut 'Press Play' draws on the syncopated, sample-based rhythms and free-associative imagery of hip-hop to evoke the tension between Britishness and Asian-ness; masculinity and vulnerability; art and life; distraction and focus. The discordant finds resolution over and over again in the chord that holds this collection together: love.

Gemma Weekes

There is a preciseness with which Haroon describes the inter complexities of love, mid-life crises and loss within his debut poetry collection Press Play. Each 'intermission' throughout the collection allows the reader to pause while still being provoked by the offerings. These poems are lyrical explorations of his life as a South Asian and neurodiverse man living in the UK right now.

Afshan D'Souza-Lodhi

We're born, we live and we die. But what of that life has been lived? The complexities and unique moments in between? Haroon's Press Play illustrates the nuances, the beautiful, the raw and the devastating moments in one's life when press play was pushed for us all. I related to this book so much and I guarantee you will too.

Rubi Alexandra

In these astonishing poems, Haroon lays bare his soul for us - from the love and romance that threatens to overwhelm him, to searingly honest appraisals of his autism and ADHD, and his place in the world. Words to make and break your heart.

Iqbal Hussain
Author, *Northern Boy*

Scenes

Trailer

Mughals
East India Company
Jinnah
Nehru
Gandhi
Bhagat Singh
Partition
Migration
Advertisements for Kew Gardens
Migration - Part 2
Cotton mills
Paki bashing
My Beautiful Launderette
Salman Rushdie
Halal meat
Beards
Angry Mullahs
Book burning
Cricket Tests
Cricket World Cup 1992
Cornered Tigers
Allah Hoo
Migration - Part 3
Anokha
Asian underground
Daytimers
Migration - Part 4
Cool Britannia
New Labour
9/11
War on Terror
Control Orders
Home Secretaries
Failed dreams
Family business
Arranged marriage
Cricket World Cup 2009
Dil Dil Pakistan
Fatherhood
Divorce
Reinvention
Autism

<8>

ADHD
Creating works of (he)art
COVID
Bereavement
Loss
Grief
Love
Love
Love
Love Takes Shape

<9>

Thoughts on "Trailer"- an essay

I am Muslim. I originate from Pakistan. In fact, to be more precise, I originate from India. That's what Pakistan was, before 1947. It was "pre-partition India" - one united country before it got split after the British ended their colonial rule. But my story begins even earlier than that, with the Mughals, the Muslim rulers who consolidated Islam in India.

The East India Company, one of the most ironically named companies in the history of capitalism, was a British company and it plundered India until it was dissolved in 1874. The looting continued under the British Raj.

India got its independence from the British and Pakistan broke away from India, all in 1947, the largest mass migration in the 20th century. Upheaval, bloodshed. Who helped us win our freedom? Jinnah, Nehru and Gandhi were the figureheads, amongst them political pragmatists and political opportunists. Flawed but dedicated to a cause. Bhagat Singh also played his part in helping us attain freedom, he was a freedom fighter. Idealistic, not practical.

I remember listening to *Immigrant* on Nitin Sawhney's album *Beyond Skin* where his dad narrated stories of how South Asians were enticed into emigrating from India and Pakistan to England with seductive pictures and words about Kew Gardens. Cue migration #2. Coming to England.

Many South Asians were encouraged to come to work in cotton mills and factories. That's the story up to the 1960s.

Enter the 1970s. "Paki Bashing". The National Front, a bunch of thugs wearing steel toe capped Doc Martins going around kicking in the heads of "Pakis". I don't hear that word as much anymore. "Paki", the racial insult for Pakistanis and anyone who generally looks "brown". But it still unsettles me when I hear it, especially when spoken at me. I think the last time was 2010. But not everyone is as lucky as me.

The 1980s were wild. *My Beautiful Launderette*, a Stephen Frears film with a brown actor on screen, a brown boy, a gay one at that! Taboos being broken. Then Salman Rushdie - *The Satanic Verses*. Book burning. Mullahs. Beards. Halal meat. It felt that was all the press and public were focused on about Muslims. It's reductive. We're more than that!

I remember Norman Tebbit and his infamous "Cricket Test". He said that if England played cricket against the country of your parents' origin and you cheered for your parents' team rather than England, you would "forever be a foreigner with a British passport."

<10>

Pakistan won the Cricket World Cup in 1992. The team chanted Allah Hoo, a Qawwali*, in the changing room when they won the World Cup. They shouldn't have won. They were battling being knocked out. But they scraped through and then fought like "cornered tigers". Imran Khan, the team's captain, coined this phrase and told his team to fight like that. It worked. Pakistan put on incredible performances in the semi-finals and the finals. And they won. As I write this, I feel it's a metaphor for my own life.

I'm still here, fighting.

Fighting to give my creativity and give my art a chance.

Fighting to figure out who I am after a lifetime of disassociating from myself.

Fighting to become the best version of myself.

Fighting to love myself and not look at others for my salvation.

Fighting to break free from narratives that haven't served me.

Cue migration #3. I faced a lot of racism in school, then suddenly a new headmaster arrived, and he cracked down on all of it. Kids lined around the block to give fearful and genuine apologies for the hurt they'd inflicted. A new start perhaps? Not the one I thought. Enjoying school minus the racism was short lived. It lasted two weeks, maybe a month. I was an undiagnosed autistic kid and my mum decided to pull me out of school and take me and my sister to Pakistan for five years. There was no conversation. No discussion. The decision was made for me. I wish I could have stayed with my father in the UK during those five years.

Living in Pakistan was joyous, but it was difficult, and exacerbated my identity crisis, as I lived and studied in a country that didn't feel like home. The thing is, England is home, but hasn't always treated some of us like we're welcome.

My father would visit during the five years and bring me magazines from the UK. Music and pop culture related stuff. I was so excited at what I saw emerging in the UK. *Goodness Gracious Me*; a British Asian sitcom, was making waves. Talvin Singh started an underground music night called *Anokha*, and the sound of the "Asian Underground" was born, fusing Asian sounds with drum n bass, jungle, dub, and every other sound that was part of the 1990s melting pot in Britain.

Nitin Sawhney was blazing a trail too. He was involved in the "Secret Asians" with Sanjeev Baskar which eventually became *Goodness Gracious Me*. He also put out an album called *Beyond Skin* which had a huge impact on me. I would go into massive (then undiagnosed) ADHD and autism-fuelled hyperfixated monologues about what that album meant to me. I even reference it in *Intermission #9* in this book.

<11>

All this was happening in the UK and I was stuck in Pakistan.

I missed England and spent most of 1995-1998 listening to British music while I was finishing up school in Pakistan. There was the obvious stuff. Oasis & Blur. I loved both, but preferred Oasis at the time. Now I look back and prefer Blur. Funny how time and age can change your taste.

But then there was Massive Attack, Portishead, Tricky, The Prodigy, The Chemical Brothers, and so many more. The common thread was the influence of hip hop in their work. You hear it in the use of samples, you heard in the drums. It's in how the drums are programmed and in how the kicks and snares are so thick.

Hip hop changed my life and introduced me to people I now call my "found family".

My maternal grandfather, or my "Nana Jaan", who I've written about in *Why Nana Jaan Had No Milk* passed away in 1997, and so in 1998, again with no discussion or reasons given, I was brought back to the UK. Despite the lack of a conversation around it, I was happy and just wanted to get back to England.

Migration #4. I moved back to the UK. This was weird. I had grown up under Margaret Thatcher and Norman Tebbit in the 1980s - that meant racism and being told you didn't belong. However, I moved back to the UK and it was 1998, one year into Tony Blair's New Labour and Cool Britannia. People were nice to me. I felt included.

It was a beautiful time. 1998 to 2000. I discovered myself. Those two years are so important because as time went on, I lost myself again. I'm still finding and rediscovering myself and that period of two years is an anchor that has helped me as I recover. But the euphoria of 1998 to 2000 didn't last. 9/11 happened and once again, like the Salman Rushdie affair, Muslims were in the news. What followed was the "War on Terror", this included "Control Orders" that were an assault on the bodies and minds of Muslims in the UK. Stripping them of their dignity and civil liberties. The architects of this madness? Home Secretaries Jack Straw, David Blunkett, Charles Clarke, John Reid…

I entered my 20s and I failed at my dreams. I surrendered. I did two things following that surrender, two things I swore I'd never do - I joined my family business, and I agreed to an arranged marriage. Neither made me happy and I walked away from both in the years that followed.

But before that, 2009 and I saw Pakistan win the TwentyTwenty Cricket World Cup. I remember when we won, it was at Lord's and they played *Dil Dil Pakistan* by Vital Signs, a Pakistani pop anthem. I wept. I can't explain the relationship I have with being Pakistani and with cricket, it's some emotional shit. My then

<12>

wife was pregnant with my only child who I have dedicated a section of this book to. I felt I was on the cusp of building a great life full of "success". I was down the road from London Business School. I had applied and felt it was my destiny to study somewhere so near to Lord's. I ended up studying there 2010-2012. And, my daughter was born in 2009. She's magic.

I initiated my divorce in 2017. It finalised in 2020. Enter COVID. It claimed the lives of two men who supported me through my divorce. Ty and my Mamu (maternal uncle) Khalid. Two men I loved deeply. Loss. Grief. I got Covid. I currently live with Long Covid.

But, through 2017 to the present day, I discovered love.

I fell in love.

I won the Tinder lottery and fell in love with someone special.

I fell in love with my creativity.

I experienced love through friendships.

I experienced love in community.

It's movement in the right direction.

I need to learn to love myself, to allow myself to be loved.

But this book you hold in your hand is a revolutionary act of self-love.

It is the first of many creative works from me that I want to share.

It is my gift to myself, and it is my gift to you.

I hope I am granted many more breaths so I can place more gifts in your hand.

Khuda Hafiz**

haroon

*A Qawwali is a style of Muslim folk music. It's religious devotional music.

** Khuda Hafiz is a phrase used to say goodbye by South Asians. It is used in Urdu, the national language of Pakistan and it literally means "May God be your protector."

<13>

Press Play To Let The Movie Begin

Get off the plane first
God rewards a bias for action
Journey across borders and continents
Tread the earth gently
Unlike those who forced us to abandon our lands
Once abundant and self-sufficient
Now chief importers
Exacerbating deficits

Get off the plane first
Then breathe in the air
Free from dust
Thick with prejudice and assumptions
Let your feet adjust
to roads paved by cold weather
and colder hearts

Make a home
laced with anxious talk of involuntary repatriation

I was born of this
Defeating anger is joyful
Resentment dissipates
My elders focused on survival
so I could thrive
Their care
intertwined with dysfunction
and neglect
Hurt people hurt people
No more looking back and dwelling
Draw a line under it
Process it
Document it
Then build
Press play to let the movie begin

<14>

My Name Is

Haroon
Not Harry
Kingmaker
Not King
To truncate a name
To amputate it
Is to amputate history

<15>

Sliding Doors

1.

Swipe left
not right
Digital sliding doors
More gaslighting
No six-hour walks along the Thames

2.

Queued for a gig
Kings X cold
sinks to my bones
One in one out policy
Nah
I'm off home
No night bus ride home
No Urban Griots
Cruising on autopilot
Mediocrity
the theme music
Turn it up to 11

3.

I paced back and forth
outside a hospital
Six months early
There was no calendar entry
warning me of a "miscarriage"
Sexless marriage ensues
No re-creation
Undiagnosed dopamine dips
keep my head below water
A journeyman who drowned
in his own lack of
purpose

<16>

4.

Cast out
Car boot full of books
and clothes
Two month back yard hiatus in Luton
Viewings in Brixton followed
Fuck you, gentrification
SW9 morphs into SW16
So much promise
However
leap of faith stalled
Opt to retreat close to English roses
Spirit slowly fades
Moleskine notepads never fill themselves
Akai MPC gathers dust
Logic remains unopened
I craft a sarcophagus for my dreams
Don't wake me up please

<17>

A Better Tomorrow

Atypical behaviour often goes unpunished
Perplexed, I sit back, questioning my own memory
Originally I blamed myself
Limiting beliefs like that anchor us in self-
abusive patterns
Of course, this happened to those who came before
me
Generational patterns stop here with me
Yearning for a better tomorrow is the driving force
to forgive

<18>

Intermission #1

Parenthood
Perplexing emotions
Navigating life
with no road map

Zaynub

Catalysed by opposable thumbs
Hips move
Hope is a groove
The future makes movement manifest in the present
This present was almost miscarried on the day of my
birth
I can think of no greater tragedy

<20>

Long Distance Parenting

When an anxious attachment style meets long
distance parenting
trouble lies ahead

I handle my own heart
with asbestos gloves
It's irradiated with insecurity

Trust and surrender lacking
Unconditional love has its own rewards
Even if I'm not the one cashing the cheques

I *wait for the wheel*
It never fails
I hold on tightly to it
It rotates
Clockwise
It drags me down through the dirt
My lack of gratitude and my amnesia
a source of shame
I wield
as I flog myself with it

I continue to hold tight to the wheel
as it finally drags me up and out into the light

Unreplied blue ticks don't last forever
My child beckons
We chat
Their ferocity
Their spirit
Their lack of filter
Their compassion for others
Better than any DNA test

I have mixed feelings
about a world
that politicises my 12-year-old
Truncated childhood
Not what I planned
for them
We laugh

<21>

We swear
Mutual declarations of love
fuel me
at a time when the cost of a litre of unleaded will
make your eyes water
I hover over travel updates
Red — Amber — Green

I celebrate equal marriage in a faraway land
They scoff sarcastically
"It's a low bar, dad!"

They remind me to reach for the stars
with fingers fully stretched
Their self-awareness
An affirmation of my choices
They remind me I am loved
They remind me I am love
They remind me to demand better from this world
They haven't yet learned to accept bread crumbs
They want nothing but the whole loaf
Crafted by artisanal hands
Infused with unconditional love

<22>

Eggs

My favourite staple
Versatile
A binding force
One minute Lauryn Hill
Next,The Fugees
I craft a peculiar omelette for my desi daughter
Slightly burnt
Garnished with green chillies
Sprinkled with seasoning
I remember her order keenly
Roles reverse
Pancakes
Fluffy
Made from the best brown-shelled eggs
Free range
Deep rich orange yolks
Satiating
Pancakes rise
She sketches my initials on mine with honey
I add a dash of lemon juice
Sweet and tart
How apt
My daughter's reciprocity
A balm I reapply
To ease the pain of separation
To overwrite that final goodbye,
at the boarding gate

<23>

Intermission #2

Pandemic
Zombie apocalypse
Aim for the head
Always
Wear masks
Don't stop breathing

31 Days

Walked
Ran
Let the sun kiss my skin
Spun vinyl
Spun tales
Wrote poems
Performed poems
Heard poems
Explored worlds
Promised to create worlds
Cried
Laughed
Prayed for friends on ventilators
Feared loss
Become fearless
Caressed an Akai MPC with my hands
hoping to recreate my palpitations
Rediscovered a love of rhyming
Fallen in love with my daughter again (several
times at least)
Celebrated my birthday
Explored love
Celebrated it
Explored lust
Consigned shame to the dust bin
Wrote another fucking poem

<25>

Intermission #3

Rapping rude bwoy
Special kind of fool
Awkward
Forever creating
Works of heart
Like you never heard before
Rapper
Beatmaker
Record digger
Food snob
Protector
Uncle
Son
Brother
Godfather
Friend (to many)

Ben(edict) "TY" Chijioke

1972-2020

RIP

Time After Time

Death
Catalyst
Alpha and Omega

Death
Impossible to outpace
Wears out souls
I walk around like Thanos
But there are no do overs
Plus my arthritis saw to it
Fingers almost impossible to snap

Death
A reminder
of the impermanence
of this world
Brings my lens
sharp into focus
Like adult reading glasses
or
ADHD medication

Death
Instils humility
Tomorrow's not promised to none of us
The second hand won't unwind

<27>

When We Move

Grief
Love
Neither are linear
Each
a dream-like state
Casting bewitching silhouettes
Last weekend
a celebration
of The Awkward boy
from Myatt's Field Estate

Lessons of love
can't be contained
spilling out
onto grotty pavements
holding up traffic
reminding the new locals
who really owns our neighbourhood

Sound crashes
through speaker cones
Throwbacks to sound clashes
Needles
explore grooves
Genre is a construct
Could heaven ever be like this?
Free
No price of admission
XX
XY
and everyone in between
When we move
Up and to the right
The whole world follows in our path
Your memory I hold close
Your absence is real
Yet
You're here
A guide
A reminder of the presence of love
I am loved
I am love

<28>

I am a reflection of the love
you afforded me
A lifeline
I'm confident
My head
always above choppy waters
Passing the torch
A story that seemed far off

<29>

Intermission #4

Baguettes and chapattis
        Love
Carbs and refined sugar
        Love
Anti capitalistic rants
        Love

Thank You (A Love Letter)

Thank you
Two simple words
Hearts expand
when uttered AND heard

Thank you to a friend
for seeing what I couldn't
and speaking up
Forcing my eyes open
with love, patience and compassion

Thank you to my daughter
for being present
Thank you for your sense of humour
Your sharp acerbic wit
makes me exclaim "oh shit!" routinely

Thank you to my lover
for giving me a yardstick to measure love by
even though love is infinite

Thank you to myself
for advocating for myself
A recently acquired behaviour
Setting boundaries and loving self

<31>

Love with Precision

You can see something with your unborrowed eyes
But only if you choose to
Filtered vision
Often the easy choice
in a world full of distractions

Strolls in my local park
take on a new dimension
Walking past plants
I notice multiple hues
Nature's billboard
Photosynthesis meets technicolour

I took on a lover
She chooses to see with unborrowed eyes
I clock her observing
My childlike wonder finally restored

<32>

Shielded

Shielded by her formidable body
excuses melt away
God doesn't give us what we ask for
but what we truly desire
How will I proceed?
Pressure reveals true character
or lack thereof
No more hypotheticals
Real time unfurls
like Dead Sea scrolls
Deciphering as I go along
Read as I write
Get out of my head
Need to get into my body
Spectrum traits
begin to make more sense
Synaptic ricochets
in 299 directions
I now follow each with ease
Her formidable body
houses a heart like no other
and a brain even Turing
would struggle to crack
Met my match
Yet confrontation free
The Iron Man suit to my Tony Stark
Superpowers finally unlocked
Convictions tested
Shielded by her formidable body
I need no longer hide

<33>

Quantised Love

You saw me
Through my eyes
I felt cherished
We embraced
Heartbeats
Like step sequencers
Quantised
My naked chest
Pressed tightly against yours
Beating in perpetuity

<34>

Intermission #5

Renewal
Growing pains
Bahaar
Spring

(Bahaar is Urdu for Spring)

Midlife Crisis

Midlife crisis deferred by a year
This is the power of love and acceptance
Fuelled by a mutual fondness of carbs and refined
sugar
Everything has an expiration date
So too does this
41
A prime number
Apt marker for my midlife crisis
Duvets can't provide cover forever
from those dopamine dips
serotonin droughts
or repressed emotions
Life
A dynamic equilibrium
Father figures transition
Offspring become less dependent
Love morphs
Shifting from romantic focal points
to platonic
Shedding my skin is painful
Yet necessary
Unavoidable
Love guides my hand on the page
Releasing grief, denial, acceptance and generosity
Ambiguity on the spectrum
Anxiety-inducing
However
I'm learning to surrender to it
My first love came and went without warning
Creative joy manifests unpredictably
What lies ahead?
Fear
Resistance
Creative abundance
This is the best chapter of my life

<36>

It's a Great Show

Show and tell
An assault course
on the path to true intimacy
Raw
Requiring daily stoicism
and trust
Masks fall effortlessly
in each other's company
Exposing broken hearts
and broken art
Risk hurtles inbound
We poke gently
Creating wormholes
Giving glimpses
into each other's past
Taking off our cool
Hanging it safely
by our jackets
Wrapping ourselves
around each other
Performing periodic double takes
Surely serendipity can't be this good
Joy
Excitement
Healthy doses of fear
The obstacle is the way
Ego is the enemy
Love is a relay race
One time I forgot to bend down
when you tied your shoelaces
Creating a chasm
that quickly
housed a vacuum
Empathy withered on its vine
But
it's spring

<37>

Daring Greatly

I watch the men and women drift out of the station
Anticipation accumulates
Like building steam with a grain of salt
I put my best foot forward
Daring greatly
Hold tight
Our story isn't over
A new act begins
A life in parts
The mask of masculinity
weighed heavily last year
A true enemy of intimacy

<38>

Growing Pains

Growing pains
come from pushing your heart
to the limit
That thing you're feeling
The discomfort
It's not anxiety
It's the heart's bat signal
Triggered by uncertainty
Excited at the promise
of a brighter tomorrow
The world is my country
My found family growing daily
We are each other's garments
You
are a shawl I wrap myself in
Unrestrained conversations
Testing ground for our bond
I broke my promise to myself
to live bravely
Our conversations
A casualty
Olive branch extended
Jump cables at the ready
I want a second chance

<39>

Love's Reflection

Hearts aren't built for darkness
They thrive in light
My patterns are disrupted
with each act of kindness
you slingshot effortlessly in my direction
I was put on this earth
to heal my broken art
through weekly scheduled sessions
A call-out to the muse

Boundaries get redrawn each time we communicate
Eid
A time to repair bridges
Oily food lubricates love
A carb and meat fiesta
Yesterday
was a watershed
I will always carry my sorrow with me
However
I'm no longer inert
I keep it moving
Head held high
Eyes locked forward
Full of wonder
I still have time
to create joy
Let it wash over me
A baptism
I am love
I am a reflection of the love you afforded me
I will keep working quietly
Present
Chipping away
at my anxiety
Smiling
Creating
Radiating life
Volatility smoothed
Allowing beauty
to take up permanent residence
in my heart

<40>

Love in 35mm

I heard what you said
Weighed each word
Each pause
Carefully
It's not enough
Behind what you said
Lie words…
…unseen
I was born without the cipher
to break through the codes
of the words you display
to view the words you hide

Your beautiful face
a rainforest
of micro expressions
Each one
tells a story
projected
24 frames a second
Your soul
on grainy 35mm film
Captivating
Momentarily pausing my ADHD
I breathe
Slowly
Deeply
Oxygenating dormant parts of my spirit

I'd have skipped this chapter
if this was a book
It's a good thing I prefer movies

<41>

My Frayed Autistic Heart

Remember
Things fall apart
You could trace backwards
to The Roots
or
delight at the challenge
of
putting the pieces
back together
Rearranged
Reinterpreted
A collage of memories
and interpretations
Everything
Everywhere
All at once
299 thoughts
Splintered
Cognitive kaleidoscope
Heart radiates love
Like a Care Bear
Pre-9pm watershed
Optimism
An operating system
Only requiring minimal upgrades

I'll come clean
when the time is right
For now
I trust you
to break bread with me
at your leisure

My anxiety
Currently at a bare minimum
A testament
to the distance I've travelled

I'll admit
My trajectory
is jarring
a Francois Truffaut-like jump cut

<42>

Traipsing around London
Sierra Whisky
Heat and humidity
Faithful companions
The thermometer lies
But
my frayed autistic heart does not
Forever calm in your presence
Home

<43>

Dawat (Feast)

Food shared
tastes just that little bit sweeter
Satiates
Never walking away wanting more
than I've consumed
Dawat
Feast
Banquet
Tooting
Coriander
Haldi
Garam masala
Ghee
South Asian cholesterol
Garlic
Ginger
Seasoning
Summer
Humidity
Condensation
Meat sizzling
Warm naan
More garlic and ghee
Lentils bathe in oil
Lamb rests
on a pillow of rice
Each mouthful
consumed over conversation
A warm embrace
The backdrop I want to share
with the lover I love

<44>

Midlife Crisis — Redux

Midlife crisis revisited (a year later)
Pick up where I left off
Self-awareness swells
Pain swells
Love and acceptance
Gifts I will furnish upon myself
Everything has an expiration date
So too does this
42
A prime number + a prime number
Apt marker for my midlife crisis
Duvets can't provide cover forever
from those dopamine dips
serotonin droughts
or repressed emotions
Life
A dynamic equilibrium
Father figures transition
Offspring become less dependent
Love morphs (again)
Shifting from romantic focal points
to platonic
Shedding my skin is painful
Yet necessary
Unavoidable
Love guides my hand on the page
Releasing grief, denial, acceptance and generosity
Ambiguity on the spectrum
Anxiety inducing
However
I'm learning to surrender to it
My first love came and went without warning
Creative joy manifests unpredictably
What lies ahead?
Fear
Resistance
Creative abundance
This is the best chapter of my life

<45>

Intermission #6

Platonic love
Found family
Lost family
Rediscovered family
LDN
SE Asia
Brotherly love

Paul

Frame by frame
You patiently explain it all to me
Blocking
Lighting
Magic
Reversals
Sequences
Beats
Scenes
Fractals
Even when my
cognitive challenges
eat into your day and night
you fold time
Sprinkle it
with generous dustings of love
Now...
You plant me down
Blindfold me
Have me find middle C
With the purpose of unlocking
the song in my heart
Love is seeing in others
what they don't see in themselves
Then showing them THAT
Baldwin levels of unconditional love
Give
Give
Give
Until you are dry
Your patient tutelage
comes full circle

I watch memories unfold
on a screen
The memories we share
are never forgotten

My prayer for you?
To forge memories inked in love
I want the ink to flow freely
Freewheeling past the margins
Bursting off of each page you scribe

<47>

Shufen aka Ring Leader of Dolphin Police

Chaotic ball of genius
Synaptic ricochets
Bring your unique beauty
into sharp focus
Bjork meets Beastie Boys
Sprinkle of New Order
to your lack of order
There is no madness to make sense of
with you
It's clear to me
What you are

<48>

Winter Rain

The beauty
of winter rain
Falling on me
Drop by drop
Caressing every fibre of my being
Redefining kindness
Each interaction
A loving baptism

<49>

Sometimes…

No Long Ting
Gatherings
South of the River
Sometimes North
Because, fuck dogma
Stylus rides through grooves
Clockwise motion
Occasionally countered
Vibrations travel
through air
Do you remember?
Bass lines (stretched)
Drum breaks
Bodies connect
to da inner self (y'all)
I alternate
Moving and swaying one minute
Another minute I'm observing
my new surrogate family
They dance
Vogue
Whack
Two step shuffle
Break
Body pop
Some more skilled than others
Each has one thing in common
Connecting to the source
Joy
Honesty
Love
Blood flowing
Stagnation, a foreign concept
A balm as I navigate reinvention

<50>

Intermission #7

Re-parenting
Self-love
Self-discovery
Autism
ADHD
Integration
A flywheel
Operating in perpetuity
God willing

Hourglass

Fist fight
Horns and halos
trade blows
Tug of war
Back and forth
Seesaw
Path forks
Doubts emerge
Chase highs?
Liberate authentic self
Or anaesthesia?
What we do matters
But
the motivation
The driver
Determines paths
Well-practised
Well-versed
in the art of self-deception
I need to tread carefully
Time is slipping
Each grain
erodes what's left

<52>

Sisyphus

On my way
Stumbling some days
Cruising on others
Often hard to differentiate
when at the centre of chaos
Either way
It's forward movement
One sunrise at a time
Rear-view mirror smashed
Deliberately
Viewfinder pointed firmly
Upwards
Onwards
Steep gradient
requires momentum
Fuck Sisyphus

<53>

Supper on the Moon

Electric synaptic pulses
Chaotic collisions
Fleeting thoughts and feelings
Dopamine dips
Mood crashing
Creating a crater around me
Trapped
Unable to climb
Steep gradient of my own making
Hyperactivity
Making me claw senselessly
at my cage

Madness
A constant companion
Heightened
Correlating with lunar cycles
A straight line to self-loathing

Breathe
Sit still
in silence
Self-awareness swells

Madness
When harnessed and embraced
The key
to unlocking my unique operating system

<54>

Eid al-Adha - Remix

He could do as little as he wanted
But he chose not to
Mental ricochet
299 trajectories
Like a scattered bag of pennies
A dead figurehead
for every sacred cow
brought to his abattoir
Ideas nurtured
and developed
in the dark room of his psyche
Self unfolding in real time
Growth
in parallel
Atypical brain
finally understood
Self-love
Evident
Calloused skin fits nicely
A gatekeeper
Necessary
Longevity is the goal
To finally marvel at the sights
Pursuit of pot of gold
finally put to rest
Won't turn it down if stumble upon it
Plan to convert it into energy
to share and disperse freely

<55>

Good Health

Is anyone not in good health?

Pause
Silence
Lubricate cogs
Omega 3s
Loading up
Slowly
Like tapes in an Atari
High octane thoughts
push through
like water
trying to break levees
Thoughts
Fluid
Taking shape

Is anyone not in good health?
I don't understand the question
Let me answer still
Depends
on what others care to share
I wear masks
very well
it would seem
Function highly
Purpose built masks do that
They shield
They obscure reality and truth

<56>

What a Week

The power of story
Beautiful
Reels of celluloid
Passing through projectors
Casting light on dreams
Moulding new realities through make believe
Softening once-hardened hearts

<57>

Relay Race

The ranks of the ancestors swell
Heart weighs heavy
Frayed at the edges
Painting a crimson trail

Departure lounge creates vacuum
Hit gym
do reps
Pass the peas
Like they used to say
Pass The Torch

Re-up on lighter fluid
Butane
Keep alive flame
Glowing embers
Never enough
A lifetime of playing defence
gave me calloused hands

Lit torches burn bright
Radiant
Warmth of countless suns

Life
A relay race
Laces tied
Breathe from my diaphragm
My existence
An affirmation with a pulse
Give thanks

<58>

Onwards, Upwards

I did not go back
Revisiting a past life
No longer a past time
Harness 299 trajectories
Spectrum coated in balm
Creativity soothes
Love heals
So much ground covered
Sneakers replaced
Pencils sharpened
Erasers unused
Pens depleted
Latent creativity
is NOT benign
Check my NHS records
for documented proof
Creativity isn't a tool
It's the whole toolkit
Lifetime guarantee
Throw receipts in the recycling bin
Never look back

<59>

Hack Life

Art
Commerce
Hope
Dreams
Silicone
Semiconductors
Alphabet
ergonomically rearranged
Front-loaded cost
Steep
Amortised
over time
Expense
Minor
Bicycle for my mind
Track and field for my dreams
2005 'til I'll never retire
Tap away
Never tapped out
Never tap out
Narnia-like portal
to another world
Fragmented communities
Aggregated
Symbol of hope
Sense of rescue
Perhaps
my fragmented
disassembled psyche
can finally
be
assembled
Seamless
No longer held together at the seams
by rusty safety pins

<60>

Tender Was Never Gonna Make It

Wish I'd known from the start
Hang on
Teleportation doesn't exist (yet)
Disassemble into atoms
Then reassemble
Hard to repeat
the same picture
Be careful what you ask for
Two things kill
#1
Desire, unfulfilled
#2
Desire…fulfilled
It's vague
Small print undefined
That's how they get you
Horn rim placed over nose bridge
I peer carefully over them
I don't wish the past
was different
Back to diagnosis
Tender was never gonna make it
Gaslit memories
attest to this truth
Diagnosis
Powerful tool
Normalise therapy
Lean into fear
Jump in
with both feet
Splash, little fishy
can you swim in the pond?
Diagnosis
Signpost
to the truth
People peel away from my side
Hurt, I'm no longer tender
I've hardened
Calloused exterior
A revolutionary act of self-love
Tender was never gonna make it
But I have made it
Cue music, please

<61>

Magic Will Snowball

Once I get out of bed
magic will snowball
at breakneck pace
My 0-60
a thing of beauty

I step out of my body
Transfixed
Step back in
Jumping out of my head
into my body
An optimal state
But it's rare
Hard for me to access
However
I'm stubborn
Call me mule
Goat
Or mighty ox
I pull my cart
without complaint
Conserve energy
Strategic
Not every ground is a battleground
War time I thrive
Peace time, not so much
It'll change
But for now...
Discerning between the two helps

Love
Romantic
Platonic
Tectonic plates
shift
Constant flux
United in grief
We cry together
Laugh separately

Pause
Adjust

<62>

We cry separately
Laugh together
Codependency
Consigned to the waste bin
Screwed up in a ball
Three-point jump shot
Perfectly poised
Smiling
Laughing with my whole body
If I knew then what I now know…
Stop it!
Be present
Hold head high
Hazel green eyes
locked forward
Can't stop won't stop
But…
Finally…
I have room for passengers
Let's all share
in a harvest for the world

<63>

Intermission #8

All About Love

Gains

Where is it?
He growls
Serenity
A placid mind
Low dopamine
Default setting
Hurtling from one day to another
Like bowling balls
on a busy Friday night
His North Star
Clear
Brain fog
299 trajectories
SARS variant
and its residue
Impediments
Choice to be made
Pack up tools
Go home
Netflix
Next to no chill
Or answer the call
The greater the forces of antagonism
The greater the protagonist
A splintered attention span
Impulsivity unchecked
Means he never quite realises
what he asked for
However,
regret never creeps in

Sunset
Sunrise
Repetition
No more Groundhog Day
Units of time
Leveraged with greater care
There is too much to lose
But even more to gain

<65>

Besharam

Besharam
Strip away layers of shame
Apply heat to inhibitions
Peel it away as it bubbles
Sully overalls
Get paint on your nose
Rehabilitation
Reinvention
Require playfulness
and a muted inner critic
A heart free from obstructions
can love generously

(Besharam is an Urdu/Hindi word for "shameless" or
"one who is without shame")

<66>

Kinetic Trajectory

Loss
The catalyst for heartbreak
Slows down velocity
Creates inertia

Recalibrating relationships
Some change
Some end
Forlorn
Bereft of hope
Dopamine doesn't dip here
It crashes
Like NASDAQ stocks
Plummeting through a bottomless pit
But
In all of this
I have myself
My will and desire
I will love again
And love morphs
It's like energy
It can't be made or destroyed
An epiphany
which set off a wave of kinetic energy

<67>

Intermission #9

Recognising reflections in the mirror
Adjusting accordingly
Pakistani
English
British
British Asian
British Pakistani
British Muslim
Anokha
Nitin Sawhney
Beyond Skin

Why Nana Jaan Had No Milk

Staring into a saucepan on lazy Sunday mornings
Milk bubbles
Aromatic
Tea leaves
Cardamom
White full-fat milk turns brown
No kettles
Liberated
From LDN's hard water
Born of this island's hardened hearts
Milk softens hearts
Softens callouses
originally hardened
in response to Partition
Once again
At the mercy of oppressors
Lecturing us on cricket tests
Colonisers innovate sport
We perfect and subvert it
The Empire strikes back
Lacquered spheres
Spun uniquely
Like my Ami Jaan's tales
Nana Jaan breaking off chapattis
soaked in shorba
Bone broth-infused goodness
Ghee clogs my arteries
Yet each morsel expands my heart
Buttered toast
Dip in doodh pati
Tea
No water
Milk-based
Pour into a saucepan
Add tea leaves
Cardamom
Boil
Tea
Remixed
Reimagined
Our oppressors lack imagination
We lack inhibition

<69>

Palms
Fingertips
Knuckles
Multiple touch points
Create percussive sounds
on tabla skins
Newham
Poetry recited
Songs sung
in Tower Hamlets
after a long day of exploitative labour
Slow crawls with Ami Jaan
Green Street
Dhaniya
Coriander
Freshly picked
Sensory overload
Folds time and space
Return back to her flat
Empty milk bottles sit on the kitchen top
No milk for my Crunchy Nut Cornflakes
I'm bereft
Unable to regulate my response and emotions
Early signs ignored
Survival prioritised
The reason Nana Jaan had no milk?
He was busy
Creating daily reminders
in his saucepan
of who we really are
Being English is not what got us here

<70>

Home

Further and further from our home
Economic migration
Mixed with quixotic adventures
Driven by wanderlust

New frontiers
Head West
or
these days
in any direction
World re-ordered
Home
A word
A concept
Increasingly abstract

We moor our boats
wherever the tide is in
Learn new languages
Subvert them
Make them our own

We're cultural mixologists
Creating musical and celluloid cocktails
Creating joy
Refracting reality
Creating life

<71>

Intermission #10

Playing an infinite game

The Decision was Unanimous

Pitching ideas
Literally
Throwing them
from the mound
At full velocity
Repeatedly
Minus carpal tunnel syndrome
Workaholism
Cynicism
Anger
Entitlement
More bitterness
than a fistful of fenugreek leaves
Tread the earth gently
Be soft in your speech
Don your technicolour dreamcoat
Remember your Lord
Glorify Him
through how you manoeuvre this world
Bench empty rituals
Bathe in ecstasy
Single ticks will double
Shift from grey to blue
Be ready to pitch good ideas
Receive them
Great relationships
and love
Centre on reciprocity
On giving
On receiving
Like protracted Wimbledon rallies
Be sure to manicure the grass
Wear loose, cool clothing
Stock up on pitchers with...
Lemonade...
That cool refreshing drink

<73>

When I Write Enough

Write enough
Time elapses
In concentric paths
Starting wide
From the largest diameter
Hypnotically moving inward
Pain
A teacher
The cold
An even better teacher
Lessons accumulate
I speak incessantly
Yet remain guarded
An acquired operating system
I never write enough
when impediments arise
Obstacles magnify in size
Fear
Failing motor functions
My limbs have seen better days
But
I reflect
as I focus on my breath
Diaphragm swells
Expelled air
shifts consciousness
Suffering is real
Yet
imagined
Life
Full of dichotomies
Love on the spectrum
A Rubik's Cube
Hard to decipher
Not unless I learn to write
Daily
Three pages
Love takes unexpected shapes
But only when I learn to write
enough

<74>

They Burned All The Books

Ideas can't be contained
or restrained
They burned all the books
But
We descend from griots
We committed whole libraries to memory
Look inward
Be patient
Everything goes in cycles
This trough
will not last
With hardship comes ease
With hardship comes ease
With hardship comes ease
Repetition is key to memory
To comprehension
Censorship
is the last resort of weak minds
and closed hearts
Practise love
with intellectual discourse
Travel to learn
Even if you have to go to China
Motion creates magic
Untether
Roam free
No tariffs
They burned all the books
Write new ones
Our minds are free
When our hearts are nurtured

<75>

Builders' Brew

Prompt start
Soho
Well-groomed
Self-care
Words exchanged
over silk in a cup
Builders' brew
Stimulant
Empathy
Kindness
Walk away lighter
Weight shed
Heart singing
in perfect key
Middle C found
blindfolded

Instincts flow freely
when facades are shed
Like snakeskin
Decaying almost instantly

The past no longer exists
Future crafted lovingly in the present
Gifting myself light passage
Spirit now fuel-efficient
ULEZ-compliant
In this world
and the next

Give praise
Bear witness
Give thanks
Say Mash'Allah
Say Alhamdullilah
Say Subhan'Allah
Smile
Brownie points
for laughing
with your whole body
Wherever you pass through
Please, please, please
Leave thick residues of love

<76>

299 explanation

I use the number 299 five times in this book. I also used it in poems that didn't make the cut for this book.

There was a period in my life where I was writing the number into as much of my work as possible. It happened after I was diagnosed with autism (August 2020) and ADHD (March 2021). I began to understand my brain and how it's wired. Allowing me to design my life better. I then went through a period where I wrote poems that referenced how I was learning to navigate autism and ADHD.

299 references the sheer number of thoughts I have racing through my head at any one time. That's what ADHD can be, it's like your brain is a web browser and it has 299 tabs open. You don't wanna know how many tabs are currently open on my web browser on my laptop! Each one of those thoughts pulls me in a different trajectory. Hence why I write about it the way I do.

Why the number 299? Well, a common trait of autism is being obsessed with numbers, which holds true for me. I've always been that way. 299 is a prime number. So, I chose that. Turns out it has significance with "Angel Numbers".

The number 299 is apparently a sign from the angels that represents adaptability and cooperation. The angels are sending you a message encouraging you to be more helpful and embrace your surroundings so you may have a peaceful time. That wasn't an intended meaning for the use of the number 299, but I'll take it!

<77>

Shout outs and thank yous!

My Creator.

Religion hasn't served me for a long time. I'm not sure it's ever served me. But I have never doubted your presence in my life. I ask that you make me an instrument for the progress and healing of others. I hope you can answer that prayer. I want that more than wealth or any other material trappings.

Ty.

Thank you for affording me love. You changed my life. You pushed me to lean into the artist in me. You gave me the gift of your time, your attention, your care. I miss you more than words can ever do justice. I promise to make good on each and every promise I made to you when we last shared a meal. Thank you for holding me in love.

Zaynub.

Thank you for making me a father. Thank you for existing. Thank you for every moment of joy I've experienced in your company. I love you unconditionally. You changed the trajectory of my life and this book owes a lot to you.

Also, big thanks, in no order to:

Mamu Khalid, BREIS, Charni, Lucy, Akiya, Rubi, Guleraana, Paul, Abdullah, Meta, JodY, SWVrthy, Chidi, Yomi Sode, Inua Ellams, Nomadic Libaxxx, Jay Kage, Rohan, Kate (Parsley), Dean Lewis, Cyndi, Christian, Karen Arthur, Mywvanwy, Sofia, Christian St Croix, Nutty P, Akor, Claire, Selina, George Lawrence, Javid, Fahad, Vanessa Walters, Gemma Weekes, Isiah Weekes, DJ Croc, Jahmale, David Mrakpor, Umbreen, JJ Bola, Rachel Long, Roger Robinson, Tre Ventour, Kareem Parkins-Brown, Samantha-Jane Ofoegbu, Dad, Mum.

<78>

Hey, it's haroon here, I can be contacted at: haroondotkhan@gmail.com

I'm available for commissions, performances and anything you can think of.

You can also find me on Instagram at:
@harooncreates
and also @speakeasywithharoon (my podcast) for all of my latest news.

I've got a website at: www.iamharoon.co which will either be under construction or fully functional depending on when you're reading this book!

<79>

<<BE KIND REWIND<<